Classroom 101

Memories of Teaching

Classroom 101

Memories of Teaching

Yolanda Vera Martínez

authorHOUSE®

AuthorHouse™
1663 Liberty Drive
Bloomington, IN 47403
www.authorhouse.com
Phone: 1-800-839-8640

Published by AuthorHouse   08/24/2012

ISBN: 978-1-4772-6022-7 (sc)
ISBN: 978-1-4772-6023-4 (e)

DEDICATION

To the hundreds of students who spent semesters
or years in Classroom 101, so that we could challenge
one another and learn together.

CONTENTS

ACKNOWLEDGEMENTS

Twenty-two years of successful teaching would not have come about without the trust and faith that so many people had in me. Thanks to:

Yvonne Turner, Patricia Fitzpatrick, Judy Ohlemacher, and Pete Larsen for opening your classrooms, so that I could student-teach at L. Cook Middle School and Santa Rosa High School.

Bob Bunting, Mike Panas, and Bill Waxman, Principals at different times in my career, for supporting my ideas, programs, and projects.

Mary Jo Renzi, for exchanging classes with me and for team-teaching. We broke the routine and learned from different approaches.

Teaching Colleagues and staff, for assisting me in the common goal of educating teenagers, especially Andy Brennan for assuring me that computers were manageable.

Mike Mouat, Danitsa Finch, Phil Weil, Jim Tonna, Amanda Newlon, Alberto Paulsen, and Emma Zavala-López—Modern Languages Department members—for being my family at work and for sharing information, materials, and a good sense of humor.

Michelle Feleay, Janyce Bodeson, Carol Delgado, Marty Hoteling, Erick Bohn, and Lori Simerly, for being the voice of the voiceless and for your efforts to improve the ELL curriculum.

Dan Villalva, for being my professional advisor and co-mentor for Santa Rosa Junior College students interested in pursuing education and media production as careers.

Fr. Gabriel Ruiz, CMF, for being my spiritual advisor.

My husband Juan; my children Chela, Cheli, Juan Jr., Rolando and Sophia; my grandchildren Mercedez, Alicia, Tomás and Matthew, for looking after my well-being and for supporting me in my profession and my personal interests. You accepted well my "other sons and daughters"—students who often shared our lives.

My grandmother, Aurora, is remembered dearly for instilling in me the desire to be of service to others through teaching—her career as well.

Mostly, thanks to God for the gift of all these people and the hundreds of teenagers who touched my life.

INTRODUCTION

In *Classroom 101*—I share my experiences of a 22-year teaching career. My students ranged from 15 to 18 years of age. They came from all cultural and socio-economic backgrounds, and they were always full of energy and youthful wisdom. All snapshots are true, but most characters' names have been changed to protect their privacy.

My Last Graduation

The freshly-mowed grass was making me cold at sundown, but I had a shawl to cover my knees. By experience, I knew what to expect.

The Santa Rosa High School (SRHS) band played "Pomp and Circumstance" for the 400+ students graduating, as they marched into the Santa Rosa Junior College running tracks. The same location is rented every year because it's adjacent to SRHS and it has enough space for graduates and their families.

My assigned seat was in the third row from the front, middle aisle, close to the podium, and the 20 students assigned to me to supervise were on my right. Families and friends of the graduates sat on the bleachers to our left and right.

It was a joyous occasion, but I felt particularly emotional that evening. It was the 21st graduation ceremony that I attended, and . . . my last. Just like the graduates, I was not going back the following year to SRHS, Room 101—my second home, but I wanted to consider the ceremony my graduation, instead of my retirement.

The student body president led the Pledge of Allegiance, followed by "The Star-Spangled Banner," performed by the school choir. Then, we heard the speeches recalling the seniors' high school experiences and their dreams for the future.

The long-awaited-for distribution of diplomas followed. What was the seniors' prank that year? It was a different, quite creative, embarrassing situation, particularly for Mr. Jim Jones, representative of the Santa Rosa School District Board of Education and parent of one of the graduates.

The first name on the list of graduates was Michael Adams. Michael, in black graduation attire and white shirt, took a few steps forward from the first row, and as he received his diploma with the left hand and shook Mr. Jones' hand with the right, he casually dropped a size 40 or so, pink bloomer and continued to the left where the photographer awaited to take his picture.

Meantime, the second name was called, and Mr. Jones, with his polished, brown right shoe, pushed the large garment aside, as he grabbed the next diploma to hand out.

Most students had with them similar garments in a variety of colors, but instead of dropping them on the ground, they started placing them on the podium, next to the microphone, where Mr. Ray Kelley, Vice Principal, was announcing the graduates' names.

He attempted to remain composed as he read the names, but it was obvious that he didn't know what to do as the bloomers continued to pile up in front of him. Luckily, they started falling onto the ground, and they were not as visible from where the guests were seated.

Students who were returning from receiving their diplomas, and the ones waiting for their turn to go up, began to inflate their well-hidden balloons and beach balls. The balls bounced back and forth over the graduating class of 2006. Students had been inspected in the SRHS gymnasium before walking over to the Santa Rosa Junior College campus for the ceremony, but administrators were mainly looking for alcohol containers and checking if students were wearing clothes underneath their robes. Yes, at a previous graduation, a student showed up drunk and without clothes under his robe. Toys were not really a concern, but they might have taken away the panties, had the staff discovered that students had them.

At another graduation, students had tortillas that started flying in all directions at an agreed-upon time during the ceremony.

Was this behavior a lack of respect to an educational institution and its guests? I thought so, but parents didn't seem to mind, for they booed at the teachers when they caught the balloons and deflated them.

Graduation pranks were only an example of what went on at the high school, where students tested the adults' intelligence and patience at all times. There were also tears, laughter, tenderness, confusion, love, and most important of all, and in spite of all, learning.

Unlike previous years, this time I was not assisting in the all-night graduation party, sponsored by the Parent-Teacher Association, and done in school, to prevent graduates from driving around and getting into accidents. I went home around 8:30 p.m., and I couldn't help to feel nostalgic as I reminisced about the job I was leaving behind. It was a bittersweet experience.

In *Classroom 101*, I want to share some of the events that became forever engraved in my mind and in my heart.

Listed first are the unpleasant experiences, so that I end my narrative of mini stories in a positive mood.

UNPLEASANT AND SAD EXPERIENCES

Come for a tour of the room of tears—*Classroom 101*. You are welcome to shed some of your own if you so desire.

Even the Strong Cry When Saying Good-Bye

After the final exams that Friday morning, Diogo walked into the classroom, nicely dressed as was his style, in white shirt with long sleeves and black pants. Every strand of his short, black hair was perfectly in place.

His girlfriend walked behind him, and she stopped half-way into the classroom. Since she had not been my student, she was simply accompanying him and had no good-byes to express. He, on the other hand, approached my desk saying in a low, trembling voice:

"Mrs. Martinez, I came to say good-bye." I stood up from my seat at the desk, and he gave me a strong hug. He held me tight for a moment, and I realized that he was crying. He was trying to hold back his tears and sobs, for the young lady was standing nearby and some other students were still in the classroom signing yearbooks, but good-byes are always traitors, even for the strong, young men with girlfriends. Diogo ended up showing his emotions. When he separated from me, with both hands he wiped his tears, and then, he said: "At the beginning of the year, I was upset with you for reprimanding me about missing school. Later, I realized that you really cared about me and my education."

My reply ensued with a simple: "I didn't notice that you were upset, and I'm glad things worked out well for you." Smiling, I added, "You are graduating!"

Diogo had been in my Spanish for Native Speakers and Translation courses. During his senior year, he started missing school, and after a few complaints on my part, accusing him of suffering senioritis, he explained that he had a job until late at night, and quite often he was too tired to attend school.

In spite of his absences, he did well in my classes, for he always made up the work and wasted no time in class. He was attentive and respectful—one of those students teachers wish they would return to take their place as teachers in the classrooms.

Gosh! I suppose I could have locked the classroom and closed the blind on the door's window to avoid interruptions, so that I could get my paperwork done, for I still had to finish grading exams, compute final grades, and . . . vacate Classroom 101—<u>my classroom</u>. Yet, every word and hug from my angels, as painful as it was for them and for me, were important. I needed to hear that my energy had not been spent in vain and that, indeed, I had made the difference in the lives of some of them, like in Diogo's. As Robert Fisher says, "Knowledge is the light that will guide us in our path," (1) and I hoped that I had shed a tiny ray over my students, so they could guide themselves in the future.

Fear of Substituting for my Colleagues

Marlene and Elva, our School Secretaries, were extremely efficient. In emergency situations, they quickly managed to find substitutes. If it was early in the morning, it was better to call the district's substitute service and find someone for the rest of the day. If it was to cover only one period or two, they called upon teachers to cover one another during their preparation time. We were paid on a pro-rated basis. The money was good, but having to use our preparation period made the day much longer because we had to stay later after school to prepare lesson plans and any materials needed for the next day.

To substitute was also difficult because of the insecurity and fear I felt upon arriving at someone else's classroom, standing in front of unknown youngsters and having to deal with everything else unknown.

One afternoon, I was called to substitute in an agriculture class. I agreed and walked to the other side of campus as quickly as I could for sixth period. A young lady introduced herself as the Teacher's Assistant, so I asked for her help in attendance reporting, and I said to her: "Please don't do any favors. Anyone who is not here should be marked absent." She assured me, "Don't worry, Mrs. Martinez."

As soon as we took attendance, the students started to walk around the classroom, in spite of having an assignment written on the board by their regular teacher.

"Please take your seats," I said.

They said that their regular teacher usually allowed them to walk around, which was possible because of the nature of the class. Nevertheless, I felt quite uncomfortable upon seeing students walking in all directions.

"Please take your seats," I asked again. Then I added my favorite phrase: "Use the time wisely. When you finish your assignment, you may do homework for other classes, and you don't have to take it home." I was hoping to restore some order.

Next thing I knew, the real test came. Two students walked out of the classroom, continued farther back on the school grounds and started climbing a wire fence that led to the street. I walked right behind them.

"Excuse me," I yelled, "I'm responsible for you during this hour, and you need to come back into the classroom right now." I walked back to the classroom, expecting them to be walking behind me, but fearing that they might not, in which case I didn't know what I would do. I didn't have a seating chart, and even if I had one, when teachers are absent, students give someone else's name and don't sit in their assigned seats.

My tone of voice must have projected authority, though, for the two students did walk behind me, back into the classroom. I could picture them laughing at my height, only 4'8", or making faces at me for asking them to return.

The last time I had called on campus supervisors to follow students who were leaving school—and we had a closed campus policy—Alfredo, the supervisor said to me:

"I can't possibly chase all students around to bring them back. If they choose to leave, they are marked absent, and the unexcused absences become cuts. Cuts are punished with detentions after school." Good argument, and in this case I didn't even know who was who, so that I could report them. Luckily, students respond to authority when the teacher is firm, respectful, and self-confident.

I Did my Part

Regarding absenteeism, I must mention that one of my frustrations as a teacher was to see young people waste their time. It also made me angry when students thought they were outsmarting school personnel and their parents by cutting classes and not being caught. So, every time I had an opportunity to report absences, I printed their attendance record, put it in a blank envelope, and disguised my handwriting on the address. That system never failed. I knew that students answered the telephone at home, and when the call was about their absences, they told their parents that it was the wrong number, but they didn't pay attention to an envelope with awful handwriting.

A direct talk to students about their absences worked at times; they figured that someone was watching. Some students changed their attitudes about missing school and others didn't, but at least I did my part. Examples follow.

Just before the last graduation, I was walking down the hallway when Josephine approached me: "Mrs. Martínez," she started, "I want to thank you."

"Why?" I asked.

"Well," she started, half-choking as she tried to continue. Then she took a deep breath and said: "When I was in the 9th grade, I was cutting school so much, but one day, you said to me: 'You have so many absences. An education is the key to your future. Don't waste it. Wake up!' I'll never forget it. I'm glad you showed that you cared, otherwise, I would not be graduating." She took another deep breath, and then she continued: "I have passed all my exams, and I'm passing all my classes." By this time, her eyes became watery, and in a whisper, she said, "Thanks!"

I gently touched her long, wavy, black hair around her face—like mothers do—as I said, also in a soft voice, "You're welcome," and I continued on my way.

Another one of my favorite stories under this title is related to Lizzy. I saw the many C's (for Cuts) in her attendance record, so I printed a copy and sent it to her parents.

Three days later, Lizzy walked into Classroom 101 when everybody else had left. She walked over to my desk softly, as if not wanting to make any noise with her steps.

"Hi! Ah . . . I . . . just want to thank you for . . . sending . . . my attendance report home," she said, biting her bottom lip and looking down. I stayed quiet. I was quite upset with her. In fact, I think I was frowning as I looked at her. Then she broke down in tears and told me what really had touched her heart.

"My parents thought I was in school, and I kept cutting and going all over the place with my friends." There was silence, except for her sniffling, for which I gave her a napkin—Kleenexes were out of the question, for the boxes didn't last long.

"When my dad read your note and my attendance record, he cried." And when she said that, she burst out weeping.

"I'm . . . so . . . sorry, Mrs. Martinez."

I smiled at her. I knew I had "won" one, and I only recommended: "Don't apologize to me; apologize to your dad. Obviously he loves you and cares about you."

Lizzy became one of my best students. She also began to work with her parents, who cleaned offices at night. After they arrived home, some time after 11:00 p.m., she still did her homework. Her attendance record and grades improved tremendously. Perhaps it was her way of compensating to her parents all the time she had wasted and the pain she had caused them.

Sadly, I wasn't always successful, since I also dealt with stubborn youngsters. The opposite of Lizzy was Lyta.

I sent Lyta's attendance record, or lack of it, to her home when she was in the 10th grade. As soon as her parents spoke with her about it, she dropped my class. If I crossed her in the hallway, she turned the other way and didn't say hello. Then, when she was a senior, she approached me:

"Do you think I can be a T.A. (Teacher's Assistant) in your second period class? I need a few credits to graduate."

Wishful thinking! I had hoped that she had improved and that she wanted to mend our relationship by showing me that she had become a responsible individual. I thought about her request for a minute. As I sat at my desk, looking at her, it occurred to me to answer:

"But you know the rules. You have to be here punctually and every day."

"Then I don't want your help," she said immediately, and grabbing angrily the paper that I needed to sign if I accepted her, she walked hastily out of Classroom 101. What kind of future will await a person who refuses to follow rules? As García-Dávila said in a poem, "Those who don't know how to start a fire will be cold," (2), but I did try to provide the wood.

Reverse Fear

Noise reigned in the school environment; it was recess time that sunny morning. Susana walked into the classroom and sat on a desk top. That she should sit on a desk top was not common for Susana, so I became concerned, and she received my undivided attention. She trusted me with the matter at hand:

"I'm scared," she began.

My immediate reaction was to bombard her with questions: "What? What did you do? What happened? What's going on?"

Once I stayed quiet for a moment, she related the story of her fears: "You see, ever since we were in middle school, there's a group of girls always harassing me, taunting me and inciting me to fight. They just told me that they'll wait for me in the bathroom. I don't want any problems."

She made a pause. I was trying to collect my thoughts, so that I could respond to the situation. Meantime, she continued: "They are exhausting my patience, and I'm afraid that if they get me tired, or if they hit me, I'm going to hurt them badly."

I remembered then that Susana was a black belt in Tae Kwon Do, and as such, she was trained to act with patience before attacking, but those girls had gone too far; that was why she confided in me. Then, it was my job to expose the information to the proper administrator, so I asked Susana to go along with me to the office.

Ms. Lindy, the Assistant Principal, listened to us and then assured us that she would deal with the problem immediately. Later, Ms. Lindy visited me in my classroom to say:

"I called the girls into my office and told them: If you only look at Susana provokingly, you will be suspended from school." Unfortunately for them, the girls were suspended from school shortly after, not because of their harassment to Susana, but because they had caused trouble to other students on campus. It never fails, "Resentment towards others is a barrier towards one's own change and development" (3).

Too bad for those girls! What were they doing during their week of suspension? What does the future hold for them? Jail? The thought frightens me. Will they ever graduate from high school? Where have the parents been all this time? Where were they?

As for Susana, I very much admired the maturity with which she handled the situation. Many students are harassed, but they won't say anything for fear of retaliation or mockery. From then on, she was comfortable in school, and she was free to tackle her heavy load of academic courses.

Given the opportunity, and having self-trust, students confide in school staff to help them with their concerns.

Preventing Mishaps

May is a month when students put themselves in danger by escaping to places like the river, but one day, I ruined their plan.

It was during recess one hot morning when Sebio walked into the classroom, wanting to speak with me. He looked concerned, perhaps even afraid.

"Some students are planning to leave school and go to the river," he said right away and almost in a whisper, bending over on my desk, as if wanting to share a secret.

"How do you know?" I whispered, too, as if wanting to accept hearing the secret.

"They'll leave after they have class with you, but I'm worried. Last time, when we went to the river, some of them drank beer, and they got drunk. Romi almost drowned. Romi is going to drive today, and he didn't even ask his brother's permission to take his car. I'm just so afraid," was his confession.

"I'll speak with Romi when he comes to class. May be I'll convince him not to go," I assured Sebio.

Of course, I smiled to myself when I heard that they waited to cut school until after they had been in my class. Was my class that important to them that they didn't want to miss it? Not really, they were simply hoping that I didn't know about their plan, so that I would not share it with their parents. Most of my students and their parents attended Mass at Resurrection Parish where I attended, so people usually stopped me after Mass to say hello and to ask how things were going in school.

When third period began, I immediately spoke with Romi.

"Some of your friends are concerned about your plans to cut school today and go to the river," I said. He looked puzzled at finding out that I was aware of the plan. He looked out the window, searching for the words to say.

"What? Going to the river? Who said that? Of course, that's not true."

Wanting to "save face," I continued:

"You will be driving. Did you ask permission at home? Last time you took some friends to the river, you almost drowned because there had been some drinking." I made a pause and then continued: "Look at it this way: You are responsible for those you take. What if you have an accident? How will you feel if your friends are in an accident and are hurt? Even worse, how will you feel if someone dies?"

He looked at me and didn't say anything, and since the class was waiting, I simply added: "It's my responsibility to warn you. You are old enough to know better, so I'll leave things in your hands."

During class, Romi looked worried. Most likely he was trying to decide what to do.

As third period ended, I stood by the door. When Romi was leaving, I said to him in low voice: "Tell them that if they leave school, I'll report them immediately."

It's good for students to have an adult in school whom they can blame for not going along with peers' ideas and silly games. They may not like the person at the moment, but perhaps some day they will decide that she did okay in intervening.

The Cry Room

Behind Room 101, there was a small room. We called it "The Cry Room" because so many times we used it for that—crying. Here are two examples of its use:

A young father, Mr. Nicolás Pérez, in his late 30's or early 40's, arrived in school, wanting to speak with me. We went into the little room in the back, and he began to cry. He had gone unexpectedly to school, looking for his daughter, and she wasn't there. The attendance record that the office gave him showed that she had missed several days, and apparently she had signed her own notes excusing her absences.

"What do I do?" He asked, but he continued talking. "We have plans to celebrate her 'Quinceañera' (a passing of age celebration for Latin-American girls), and now I find that she is not in school. I am so sad . . . so angry!"

The minute he said that, I knew what my advice would be.

"You are celebrating her Quinceañera?" I asked in an unhappy, sarcastic voice, mixed with an expression of disgust and disappointment. Then I continued to explain:

"A Quinceañera is to celebrate life, but the celebration stresses responsibility. The child becomes a young lady who is an asset to herself, the family, and the community. She is where she is supposed to be, doing what she is supposed to be doing," I said to Mr. Perez. "Obviously, you have nothing to celebrate, for Arminda isn't even in school." Mr. Perez kept on sobbing, with his hands clasped together, and his elbows on his knees.

"I suggest you take away what she likes, like television programs and her telephone," I said, "until she shows you a good attendance report, good grades, and a good sense of responsibility in everything she does." Silence!

"School is her only job, and if she is not attending, you have nothing to celebrate," I said, trying to emphasize his need to correct the situation.

"But . . . everything is ready; the church, the hall, dress, and all," he said, crying and now, covering his face.

"Well, Mr. Perez," I said, raising my voice a little, "everything can be cancelled if you so decide."

He left The Cry Room, and frankly, I didn't want to know if he proceeded with the festivity. I would have been more embarrassed to have a celebration of an irresponsible daughter than to cancel it. In fact, Arminda's friends might have learned a thing or two about responsibility if her father had decided to cancel the party.

Not only parents with problematic students went to The Cry Room to vent their desperation, but there were young ladies with cheating boyfriends as well.

Lillian entered crying desperately. Her companion and friend was holding her from the arm and walking slowly. I thought she was physically hurt, but in between sobs, she said:

"My boyfriend has left me for my best friend. That's what hurts. With so many girls around, why does he have to pick my best friend? And she knows I love him. Why is she taking him away from me?"

"Goodness! What do I say to her?" I thought to myself, blinking my eyes and looking at her. It was lunch time, I had not finished eating, and fifth period would be coming soon. Time was always the worry in school. There was never enough time for anything, yet unexpected situations had to be fit into the schedule.

"Your boyfriend left you for your best friend." I paraphrased her problem. "Then, your boyfriend doesn't deserve you, and your best friend is not even a friend," I said, stressing my words. I was seating with my legs crossed, resting my hands on my lap. As I looked for words of comfort, it occurred to me to say:

"I have a feeling that two months from now, you'll be laughing at having cried for him." Those were the magic words. The friend, who had remained quiet, moved closer to her, put her hands around Lillian's shoulders and comforted her:

"Yeah, remember? Not long ago you were crying because . . ." I didn't pay much attention to the whispers between them, but I knew that something similar had happened before, and the situation was under control when Lillian, in spite of her red nose and teary eyes attempted to smile.

"Here," I said as I handed them passes for the next class. "When you feel well enough to go to your next class, just go." Fifteen minutes or so into fifth period, they walked out. Another problem had been resolved.

Why would a teacher in her right mind take the time to listen to nonsense like this when there's so much work to be done? Because these matters that seem nonsensical to adults are critical to teenagers. Losing one's boyfriend/girlfriend to a friend is a serious injury to the heart during that phase in one's life. We remember, don't we?

Cheating on Examinations

Every time I gave students their first examination of the school year, I preceded it with the following speech: "An unforgettable incident that I want to pass on to you today is about cheating on exams.

"I was a secretary at Sonoma State University, School of Natural Sciences, and one of my responsibilities was to help type letters of recommendation, for students interested in pursuing a medical profession. That's why I know what happened that day.

"A student who wanted to be a laboratory technician was caught cheating in a lab exam. His file was sealed with the exam inside and a document explaining in detail what had happened. Sad!

"Could we trust a cheater with drawing our blood? Could we trust the results of a laboratory blood test done by a cheater? No, in many cases our lives depend on the results of that blood test.

"I'm not saying that all of you are going to be laboratory technicians. But, can we trust a person who cheats, regardless of the profession?

"Well, then, in my exams, I don't want to catch anyone cheating. Get a B or a C that is yours and be proud of it. Don't get an A that is not really yours. Are there any questions?" Then I distributed the front-to-back printed page.

I figured that after my speech, I could concentrate on grading chapter assignment packets that students had turned in prior to the written test. Wrong!

The entire classroom was quiet in that Second-year Spanish class taking a written exam on chapter 1 of the old *Plazas y Paisajes* book. All we could hear was the normal sounds of writing tools and the sniffling of a student or two, as it's usually the case in every class.

Suddenly, Andrea stood up from her seat, walked over to my desk, threw the exam on it and said aloud: "Here. I was cheating on the test, and I remembered what you told us about cheating. I'm ashamed of myself. Give me an F."

The rest of the class looked up astonished for a few seconds, but they remained quiet and quickly returned to the task of translating words and phrases into the target language and writing short paragraphs using specific grammatical conjugations.

"Let's talk about it after class," I whispered to her. "Start working on the homework assignment on the board." I didn't think she could concentrate; neither could I by this time. What was I going to tell her after class? Even after teaching for years and years, there's always a new question, a new statement, a new incident that puzzles the mind of an educator.

About five minutes before the end of the period, I said, "Time is up. Please pass the tests forward quietly." After the rest of the class had departed, I turned to the student with brownish hair, round face, nicely dressed with a long-sleeve blouse and long skirt. I said to her:

"Andrea, it took a lot of courage on your part to stand up and say that you had been cheating on the test. Study, review, ask questions, but don't cheat. Be good to yourself. I have a lot of faith in you." She moved her head down, then up again, and she briefly looked at me. I could tell in her sad eyes that she was truly sorry. "Go now, and don't forget to do your homework." She nodded her head and walked out in long but slow steps.

I could not believe what I had witnessed in that class, but I surely found out that some of my students were listening to me and that my words were making a change in their behavior for the betterment of their future. And, she probably taught a good lesson to the rest of the class. "Most . . . teachers work continuously to liberate limitations . . ." (4). In this case, Andrea had been liberated from not having enough confidence, to the point that she had to resort to cheating.

Pre-Conceived Ideas and Discrimination

Regardless of how much effort most academic students place in expressing their appreciation and respect for people of other cultures, there's always one in each group who ends up showing misinformation or prejudice.

Before starting my lesson about "The Hispanic Culture" and what "Culture" entailed, I asked my Third-year Spanish class: "When you hear the word 'Hispanic,' what comes to your mind?" There were answers naming the entire menu of Mexican food restaurants: Tacos, burritos, enchiladas, and more. After a few seconds of silence, a student raised his hand and said: "Fat, brown babies." I smiled and asked if there were other ideas. There certainly was another one when Nila said: "Dirty people. I have never seen a clean Hispanic person."

The only thing that occurred to me was to bow and say smilingly: "Thank you."

The rest of the class responded in a variety of ways: Some covered their faces in disbelief that an academic student at this level of foreign language education should say that, and that she should say it to the teacher who was Hispanic. Others made sour faces. One young lady said: "Come on!"

"What?" Asked Nila, looking around, trying to determine why the other students had reacted to her comment the way they did.

"Mrs. Martinez is Hispanic," Paul said, and with her eyes widely open, Nila carried her hands to her mouth and shrugged her shoulders. "Oops!" She exclaimed.

"Damas y caballeros, continuemos—Ladies and gentlemen, let's continue," I said, as a transition to the topic of the day.

At one time or another, we all discriminate against others for their looks, socio-economic status, education level, and cultural background. If at home such behavior is accepted, and perhaps even generated, what can we expect? Some people forget that in each culture there are the intelligent, dumb, outspoken, quiet, rich, poor, educated, ignorant, ugly and beautiful. We need to start treating people as individuals and not as races in general, so that we don't make "dirty" comments that embarrass those around us.

Parents—the First Teachers

We often hear that the first teachers of children are their parents, and that sounds reasonable. They teach them their first words, help them to take their first steps, and they teach them manners. We just wish that more parents would do at least that.

School teachers will agree that when children have been taught at home their simple, every-day manners, such as saying "please" and "thank you," those children will display their manners in the classroom and wherever they happen to be.

Even when parents have taught their children proper behavior and teachers have reinforced it, some youngsters decide to take the wrong turn. Cain fits well this description.

It seemed that every Monday Cain arrived with a heavy story:

"Saturday night I blew up the mail boxes in my street," he would say with a big smile.

"This morning, when I was leaving my house, I ran over a cat," he said another day.

I tried to listen to each student who entered Classroom 101, so Cain felt free to walk in first thing in the morning to talk, although he didn't have class with me until later in the day.

At first I thought he was watching too many horror movies, and since he spoke with a smile, I thought he had a bad, cold sense of humor. But to be on the safe side, I filled out a Referral Form and sent it to his counselor. Along with it, I sent a letter giving examples of the stories Cain was telling me.

Two days later, the counselor replied: "Don't worry. I had a talk with Cain, and it seems that he is only making up stories."

Imagine my surprise and sadness when one day I read in the newspaper that he had killed an elderly couple by the coast in Sonoma County. As a result, he is spending the rest of his life in prison. Could I have done more? Probably, but I don't know what. Obviously, his first teachers could not help him either.

Some Parents are the Greatest Problem

An entire book could be written only on the subject of parents as the greatest problem, but I will limit my comments to the following examples:

Lola, a tall, thin, beautiful young lady with long, curly hair, was one of the first students to arrive to class every day and immediately take out her materials.

She impressed me when the Friday before Christmas vacation, she asked: "Do you have the complete book, *Don Quixote de La Mancha*?" We had just finished reading a condensed version of Miguel de Cervantes' novel. My answer was positive.

"May I borrow it? I would like to read it during vacation," she said.

Cheerfully, I went to the cabinet—a student wanted to read more! And she wanted to read it over the Christmas vacation! I handed her my copy of the requested book.

Lola was an A student. Her written and oral assignments were cleanly presented and thoroughly written. In fact, she was the Editor of our Spanish monthly magazine, "La Voz de la Juventud—The Young People's Voice." I knew she would be successful in life.

In the second semester of her senior year, I suddenly realized that I had not seen her filling out any college applications, and opposite to many of my senior students, she had not asked me for a letter of recommendation.

"I won't be going to college," she explained when I approached her about it.

"Why?" I asked, wrinkling my forehead and keeping my mouth open in surprise.

"My mother has decided that I should marry my neighbor. She has decided that he would make a good husband, and she wants to have grandchildren soon," she explained.

The mother and I had a few discussions about Lola's grades, her intellectual capacity, and her brilliant future if she attended college. Nothing convinced the mother.

Luckily, Lola attended Santa Rosa Junior College, and the teachers and counselors of the Puente Program managed to transfer her to the University of California, Los Angeles. Nevertheless, Lola had to go without her mother's blessings, and her mother refused to speak with her again. Even when she graduated with a double major, Anthropology and Spanish, her mother still refused to go to her graduation.

On top of that, I couldn't attend her graduation either; my son, Juan, was graduating from Santa Rosa Junior College the same day.

Another problem with a parent was when we were going to the University of Santa Cruz. The day before the field trip, Petra said: "My father refused to sign the permission slip. He said that we and the teacher are just going to goof off."

That statement made me angry. While the student was standing by my desk, she gave me her home telephone number. I dialed it and spoke with the father.

"It's okay to say that you don't want your daughter to go on the field trip," I said angrily, "but to say that I am going to goof off with the students is a terrible offense to my dedication, and I will not tolerate such comments."

He apologized and, of course, that evening he signed the permission slip. But, why did I have to waste so much energy with parents' behavior? Didn't I have enough with the students'?

How about the Romero sisters who had to get married in order to continue their education? María, the oldest, was a student with a thirsty mind. English was her second language, but she asked to be placed in Academic English. The teacher said to her at the start of her sophomore year: "You don't belong here. You'll get an F."

When she told me about the teacher's immediate prediction—more of a discriminatory statement by the language he used—I immediately thought of recommending her to another teacher, but María said: "I am going to stay there. If Mr. DeSanto gives me an F, at least I'll have learned what academic students learn." Well, Mr. DeSanto ended up admiring her for accepting the challenge, and he helped her succeed in his class.

A few weeks before her graduation, she announced: "I'm getting married."

"What!" I yelled, as I gave her a questioning look.

"Well, my parents don't want me to go to college, but my boyfriend is willing to allow me to continue my education if we get married," she said calmly, as if she had studied the situation carefully.

I was feeling that my mansion, her mansion, and all our efforts for her to succeed were tumbling down. "Nooooooo!" I screamed. She calmed me down when she said:

"The agreement with my fiancé is that he will allow me to attend college, or I will not marry him. It's okay. It's the only way that I can continue my education. Otherwise, I have to live with my parents, find a job right away, and forget about school. They'll still have total control of me, and I don't want that to happen."

María did get married after graduation from high school. Soon after, she became pregnant and had a baby boy. However, her husband kept his promise of supporting her in her education, not only economically but also by taking care of the baby while she was in school. A few years later, she received a B.A. in Business Administration from Sonoma State University. It must be true that, "The goal of marriage is not to think alike, but to think together" (5) and support each other, like María and her husband did.

Maria's younger sister followed the same path, and by then, their parents realized that they were making a mistake in not allowing the girls to be educated. The parents changed their minds, and then the mother offered to at least baby-sit for them while they went to college and to work.

The Saddest Day in my Career

That sunny morning, I arrived in school at 7:30 a.m. as usual. Reflecting my confidence and professionalism, I firmly walked up the steps that led into the main building, through the back door, from the faculty parking lot. Classroom 101 was the first one on the left, but although I had the key in my hand, I did not get to unlock it. Ms. Felicity, a counselor, was waiting for me at the door, and she immediately took me by the arm and led me down the hallway and into the Faculty Dining Room (FDR). As we walked, she began to speak:

"I want to talk to you about Fer," she said.

"Fer, my nephew? What happened to him?" I inquired as fear began to invade me with the mystery I had encountered so early in the morning.

"No, not Fer your nephew; Fer your student, the one who transferred out a few days ago," she explained.

Yes, Ferdinand, a quiet and respectful student with a quick smile and a hat on his head all the time. He had transferred recently to Montgomery High School.

When he asked me for his grade in my class and my signature on the document for the transfer, I thought to myself: "He lives closer to that school, so it'll be good for his family not having to come all the way over here." I returned the form to him as I said:

"Good luck to you! Keep up the good work!"

I should not have assumed that I knew why he was transferring. I should have asked him why.

Apparently a group of students was harassing him at our school, wanting him to join a gang. In an attempt to protect him, his family had decided to send him to Montgomery, where he was supposed to attend in the first place, but I only found out this information after the regrettable incident that was being revealed to me that morning.

"Fer committed suicide," said Ms. Felicity as we entered the FDR.

I noticed immediately groups of students around the room, most of them crying, and those who were not, were looking at the walls in deep concentration. The girls sobbed and whispered among themselves about the circumstances that may have prompted Fer to end his life.

Ms. Felicity had taken me there in case I needed help from the special counselors that had been called for assistance, but I realized that at that particular moment, I needed to be strong.

"I'm going to my classroom," I said to her. "Someone may be looking for me." Indeed, as soon as I entered, students began to crowd in there as well. Classroom 101 was the homeroom to many students.

All we did in my classes that day was to talk about what had happened. As the day progressed, we had more details. Whether they were right or wrong, we found out that: The day before, Fer had gone to Spring Lake with his girlfriend. He returned home very late, and his parents were worried and quite upset. His father spoke to him harshly. That, plus the other details of changing schools and who knows what else, made him take a cord and hang himself from his bedroom window. When he wasn't coming out of his room that morning, his brother checked on him and found him dead.

What followed were the questions about what I could have done to avoid the situation. Why didn't I ask him why he was leaving us? Why didn't I take the time to listen to him if I really wanted "to save them all" as I often said? There were so many unanswered questions in my mind. My excuse: "Ferdinand never looked worried. He always shared a smile and diligently did his class work. I could never have imagined that he had problems."

Fer most of the time wore beige pants, a white shirt, and a complementing tan hat. In my class, whenever he finished his work, he opened his drawing pad and quietly did work for his art class. When he looked up, he always had a smile to display, as if the entire world was joyful and he enjoyed life to its fullest. That was why I wasn't surprised to see so many young people at the funeral a few days later. I'm sure some of them must have been the ones trying to make him take a different path, but most of them were there because of his friendship and respect toward everyone.

His was one of those cases when a person feels so lonely among the bunch, and Van Zeller must be right when he says: "The soul hardly ever realizes it, but whether he is a believer or not, his loneliness is really a home sickness for God," (6) and Fer decided to be lonely no more.

Yes, unfortunately, in my 22 years of a teaching career, I had to attend two funerals of students who committed suicide and another one of a young lady killed in an automobile accident.

Dying is part of life. We know that we all have to die, but death is something for which we are never ready. It's a mystery we don't understand and, therefore, we find it difficult to accept. Funerals are painful experiences when those who die are close to our hearts—like Fer.

I Couldn't Save Them All

The Principal, Mr. Waxman, saw me standing outside my classroom after recess one morning, trying to compose myself before starting my class. "What's wrong, Yolanda?" He asked with concern. "I can't save them all," I said almost in tears. "Well, of course you can't save them all! Your job is to open the classroom and teach. Students need to enter and listen to you."

Those words comforted me many times, when after my support, help, and words of encouragement, some students still went on the opposite direction.

In all my years of teaching, I was assigned four to five preparations a day, student clubs, parent groups, plus the regular department and school committees. My load was unusually heavy, probably because I was the only Latina in the faculty for many years, so I was called upon to be a translator/interpreter and to do other assignments not listed in my contract. Yet, none of the work tired me as much as knowing that students had wrecked their lives, and they were so young.

Children need more than food and shelter. They need love, attention, someone to listen to them, and someone to encourage them. Even so, we just can't save them all.

Peer Pressure

Unbelievably so, all students with whom I worked wanted to succeed in life. In their writings they exposed their eagerness to progress and their dreams for the future. The statement I read most often was: "I want to be somebody in life." Yet, in front of their peers some disrupted classes, made fun of their teachers, cut classes, and were very rude. Obviously, besides peer pressure, those students had other issues to deal with, such as broken homes and, therefore, a lack of support and encouragement from their parents. Unfortunately, some took the easy way out by ignoring their own judgment, paying more attention to peer pressure, and allowing the negative aspects of their lives to triumph over the positive. The reality is: "The future belongs to those who believe in the beauty of their dreams," (7). I always wondered what would become of the youngsters with no vision for the future.

"Use your time wisely!"

SILLY MATTERS

Ted Jumped Out Through the Window

I "graduated" with 22 years of teaching experience. Supposedly, I had total control of my students. Well, how in the world did Ted jump out the window?

Chofi and I were were talking after school one day, and our conversation became quite interesting when she said:

" . . . the day when Ted jumped out the window."

"He jumped out of my window?" I asked, stressing the word "my". "When?"

"The other day," she said calmly, smiling, as if saying, he fooled you.

"Was I here?" I asked, hoping that for some reason I had stepped out of the classroom if that, indeed, happened. Or even better, hoping it had not happened.

"Yes, you were here," she affirmed with words and nodding her head.

Chofi pointed at the last of six large windows toward the back of the classroom. I went there to look down. Classroom 101 has a basement at street level, which means that the first level where the classroom is located is at the height of a second floor, and in an old school building, it's pretty high. The thought of a student injuring himself upon jumping down gave me the chills. Yes, it is possible for students to come up with the craziest things to do, just to prove to themselves and on-lookers that they can outsmart the teachers. Ted did a good job of outsmarting me.

"Did he come back?" I asked.

"Yes, he entered through the door," she explained.

Attendance reporting was the only time he could have carried out his plan, for attendance was done in the computer, and I had my back turned to the students.

Ted was a semi-quiet young man, with a quick smile, hard-working student, interested in receiving all A's in his work. He dressed neatly, and his blond hair was parted on the side. It never occurred to me that he would attempt to leave the classroom without my permission, much less to exit through a window.

Thinking that, luckily, he was fine, I decided not to take any action. The incident, after all, had happened a few days before I became aware of it. The rest of the class must have had a good, quiet laugh.

I wonder what other things students did that I never found out about. Young people certainly have plenty of energy and ideas, not to mention the valor to take risks.

Sharing Lunch and the Whole Tostada

María Felix used to eat lunch in my classroom every day. Whatever she had to eat, she would share with me, so I started sharing my lunch with her as well. She was living only with her older brother, so I was the mother figure in her life for the time being. As a result, she started saying, "La maestra and I share everything."

Four years of high school transform a teenager into an adult, and one day in her senior year, María Felix arrived after school with a good looking young man, and this was her introduction:

"Mrs. Martinez, this is Manuel, our boyfriend."

She caught me by surprise, and I blushed as I shook his hand. We both laughed at our inside joke of sharing everything, but in reality, I wanted to hide that day.

Rosita entered the classroom at lunch time.

"What are you doing?" She asked about the obvious; I was eating.

"I'm having lunch," I answered. "I'm eating a tostada with refried beans."

I broke my tostada into two pieces and asked her:

"Would you like some?"

"Yes, thank you," she said, grabbing the piece of tostada and my bean container. She ate savoring my food with so much pleasure that I knew that was the end of my lunch. I simply thought: "She was hungry."

I could tell there were students whose mothers got up early to prepare them a lunch, but they looked into the bag, ate what they liked and threw other items away. When I saw them doing that, I asked them to leave apples, oranges or juice containers on my desk. Usually there was someone without a lunch or still hungry, and he could always help himself to what others didn't want. Eventually, students learned to leave unwanted food on my desk. This practice helped students who stayed after school for tutoring or waited around to be picked up. Most teenagers are always hungry because they are active, and they are growing.

Only on Fridays I joined some of my colleagues in the foreign languages lab to eat lunch. At the entrance there was a large table where we placed our edibles, and it was some type of pot luck luncheon. Lucky for me, my classroom was next door, and the regular lunch eaters there were responsible individuals who cleaned after themselves and took good care of the classroom. Just to make sure things were okay, I would leave the door open, and that way I could hear what was happening.

Room 101 and the Display Window

Having belonged to the Art Department, Room 101 was equipped with a display window, which I inherited when I pleaded to have the room.

It was a long classroom with large tables and long cabinets along the walls. Everything was painted in a pale green that with age—perhaps paint from the 1800's—looked paler.

I begged the principal to allow me to use it when my original classroom, Room 134, became the Business Office and the Art Department moved into a temporary building.

The principal assigned me the room, and I painted everything with a surface—cabinets, heater, and walls—in a cinnamon color. You know what the joke was among staff members? One afternoon without thinking, Teresa, the cleaning lady, said:

"Good afternoon, Mrs. Brown." Then she blushed and didn't know what else to say. I looked at her with a questioning look, and she confessed: "You see, since you have painted everything brown, people call you Mrs. Brown." I thought it was funny and laughed, shaking my head in disbelief.

Eventually, Room 101 was remodeled, dividing it into a classroom with regular student desks, white boards, and a smaller room in the back. The original purpose of the smaller room was to set up computer stations in it, but with the economic problems that schools always face, the room had computer connections, but we had no computers, and if we had had them, we would have needed a paid classroom assistant or another teacher to supervise it. Therefore, it was used for my student club officers to make information posters, for students to practice skits, for preparing display items, or . . . to cry, as I already explained.

Next to The Cry Room was the display window, with its old and scratched glass. It wasn't updated during the remodeling. It was probably also from the 1800's when the school was built, but it was special. The Art Department had displayed students' creations there, and when it became ours, meaning the Modern Languages Department's, the decorations were changed every month, according to the holidays or special occasions.

We displayed writings, poems, flowers, piñatas, and all types of students' creations.

In June, we filled the window with posters about "My Successes this Year". For some, successes were matters like improving attendance and grades. Others, of course, wrote about the colleges that had accepted them and where they would be attending in the fall semester. We also displayed information about the scholarships and recognitions that the students had received. Students felt good about displaying their successes in the display window. Being in the main building, many people who went by saw them.

Regarding the display window, you won't believe the silly thing that I did.

Adi, my helper, asked, begged, that I allowed her to sit in the display window. I said, "No, you could suffocate in there, it's all enclosed except for the narrow door through which we enter to decorate." Since she was one of the students who helped me decorate it, she insisted: "See? We stay in there for 20-30 minutes when we decorate. Why can't I sit in there for three minutes?" Since she put it that way, I allowed her to sit in the window. A few minutes later, she came out bursting in laughter. "I moved when some girls went by, and they got scared," she said. "They went back to look at me again, but the second time I remained still, staring at them. They freaked out," she said.

Adi was my Classroom Assistant, so she deserved to have a few minutes of fun. Young people are good at demanding their rights, among many other things. And then, there are teachers who give in to silly matters.

Confusion at its Best

Rafa had recently arrived from Mexico with no knowledge of English. He had a thin build, wore neatly arranged clothes, mainly in brownish colors. His enlarged face with a beginning-to-appear mustache always displayed a smile. His wavy hair was perfectly combed back. Rafa simply had a warm personality that made people like him right away. Soon I named him "The Politician" because he greeted everyone and waved at everybody.

One morning, at brunch time, he was standing at my classroom door when a young lady arrived looking for me. Someone had sent her to ask me a question.

Thinking that I did not speak English, she grabbed the hand of the friendliest person around—Rafa—and led him to my desk where I was, so that he would translate for me.

"Ask her if she received a copy of this paper," she instructed him.

He smiled at her and then smiled at me.

"Ask her if she received a copy of this paper," she said again, waving the paper in front of him.

He smiled at her and then smiled at me again.

I was having fun, quietly observing the situation, and after Rafa was asked for the third time to ask me if I had received the paper, he inquired:

"What is she saying?"

"She wants you to ask me if I received a copy of that document," I said in Spanish, pointing at the document in the young lady's hand.

Rafa's smile faded away, and he looked at me with a frown, trying to figure out what was going on. The young lady didn't know what else to say or do, so she decided to go away. Of course, I wanted to know the content of the memorandum, but I figured that if it was important, it would be sent back, perhaps with someone else with better sense.

When life is hectic, it's okay to have fun with minor incidents.

Students' Infatuation

Dealing with infatuation is a serious matter for any profession, but it is especially difficult for high school teachers who have to see their admirers every day. Although I was in my mid 30's when I started teaching, I must have looked young; male students didn't waste an opportunity to express their feelings.

For a period of time, an Anglo student named Theo and a Latino student named Mando competed for my attention. One would come in during recess to leave a shiny apple on my desk, saying, "For you," with a big smile. Then the other one would come in, move the apple aside and place his where the first apple had been.

Concentrated on whatever I was doing, I simply said, "Thank you," without glancing at them. Noticing my indifference, Theo decided to be more direct. He arrived one day, went directly toward my desk and knelt by my side.

"Are you married?" He asked. I was surprised with his question, and raising my eyebrows, I answered emphatically, "Yes, I am."

"He must be the happiest man in the world," he commented and stood up. I simply made a face at him and told him: "Cut it out!"

Theo and Mando gave me the apples and cartons of orange juice that they obtained in the cafeteria. Little they knew that they were doing a favor to other hungry students who consumed them later in the day.

A few years later, I was at Sonoma State University, and I saw Theo sitting in the hallway. He must have felt embarrassed about his silliness in earlier years because he looked down when he saw me approaching. I simply said, "Hi, Theo. How are you?" and continued on my way.

My Twin

Amanda, my colleague, and I liked very much to participate in student activities and spirit days. Student Government had twin day, which meant that two people dressed alike and they were twins for the day.

My twin was blond, with blue eyes and about three inches taller than me. I am brunette, with black hair and brown eyes, but we were dressed the same, so we were twins. At lunch time, we were standing in the hallway, and Amanda asked a student:

"Can you tell us apart? Can you tell us apart? Ha? Ha?"

The young man looked at us, remained quiet for a minute, and then gave us an answer:

"No, I can't tell you apart. You are equally silly!"

Mr. Stone's Joke

Students had a tamale sale one day, and Mr. Stone, a science teacher, asked if he could pay us the next day because he didn't have money with him. Of course, I said yes, and he took his tamales.

The next day, during one of my classes, he walked in, handed me the money and looking at the students, he said:

"She paid for the beer last night. I'm reimbursing her."

He left me speechless, walked out laughing, and the entire class had a good time teasing me, too.

"Humor lightens the load of serious work."

JOYFUL EPISODES

So far, I have been writing about sad moments, and silly experiences, but some of my lasting memories have to do with happy experiences, which made teaching worthwhile, as we will see in the following short episodes.

A Concert for me

I was arriving to school one morning when Kevin saw me and ran to meet me in the parking lot. He was one of those students who participated in many programs, so he arrived in school around 7:00 a.m. every morning.

"Mrs. Martínez, will you come to listen to me play?" He asked, clasping his hands, as if saying, "Please".

Kevin was one of the most polite and friendly students I had in my teaching career. Even if I had been in a hurry, his request had priority. It's not every day that a student offers to play just for me, so I said to him: "Yes, of course, I will listen to you play."

We proceeded to the Music building where other students sipped their coffee or hot chocolate, sitting on the floor. I walked with my school bag in hand, following Kevin, who led me to the music classroom. Once there, he took his music sheet out of his back pack, sat on the bench at the piano and was ready to perform.

I set my bag on the floor and made myself comfortable by placing my crossed arms on his piano and listened to him play. As he played, he swayed his body back and forth, at the tempo of his music. When he finished, I applauded.

"Thanks for playing for me," I said with the biggest of smiles. "It was beautiful!"

"Thanks for listening," he said, bowing his head as the great musicians do; he certainly was one.

I walked over to the other building thinking: "I get paid for doing what I like to do. My job gives me happiness and pleasure."(8).

The Lovely Llama Visited me in School

Due to my petite stature, shortly after I started teaching, I began to suffer shoulder pain, which was due to stretching too much when writing on the board. I happened to mention my problem to the students, and they bought me a brand new overhead projector. Not only did they buy the projector, but volunteers took turns in cleaning the plastic sheets that I continually used.

By using the projector, I was able to write facing the students, and by facing the students, I could see to my right the window on the door.

That particular day, I saw a friendly face standing right outside my door. It was Rhonda who had graduated two years before. She had been my student in Third-year Spanish. She beckoned me to go outside, so I finished my sentence and said to the students:

"Excuse me for a minute, please."

Oh, goodness! What was that? A beautiful, white animal was standing in the middle of the hallway. And how was it allowed to get into the building?

"I brought my llama," said Rhonda, "I wanted you to see it."

"Well, thank you," I said still quite surprised. As I advanced toward the animal, she warned me:

"You may pet her, but watch out. If she doesn't like you, she'll spit at you."

I had to stretch a little to touch her head. The llama stood straight, as if feeling conceited, looking down at me with alert eyes. She did let me touch her and didn't spit. What an experience! To think that a previous student of mine thought of me and went to the trouble of taking her pet to school, so that I could see it made me feel very special. I did have a class waiting for me, so I said to Rhonda:

"Thank you very much for bringing your llama to say hello. I'm sorry that I can't spend more time with you and her."

"Here," she said, handing over to me a handful of the llama's hair. "I saved it for you." She gave me a quick hug as she said good-bye and pulled the llama away. I tried hard to concentrate in my lesson once I walked back into the classroom, but I kept thinking about the special treat I had just received. When I went home that evening, I made a pillow for my little statue of Baby Jesus with the llama's hair. Every time I see it, I remember dearly the day when Rhonda and her llama visited me at school.

Life smiled at me one more time!

Music—a Teaching Tool

Students in Spanish as a Second Language loved to sing. There was something special about singing in a foreign language. Once I grabbed my guitar, especially on Fridays, students thought that they didn't have to work. The truth was that in singing, they had to produce syllables and words in a faster fashion, helping them improve their pronunciation and oral communication.

Some of my happiest moments were when my students joined my colleagues—Mary Jo, Danitsa, Phil, Amanda, and Machiel—and me during school cultural activities. We joined our voices and guitars to produce the sweetest of melodies. Students were excellent guitar players. They must have been in Kevin's music class. Then, as video cameras became accessible in school, we recorded our activities, like Cinco de Mayo, and we viewed them later, re-enforcing the students' production of the so-called "Target Language".

Did I say that the school had access to video cameras? Well, in my last few years on the job, we had access also to the Community Media Center (CMC). The CMC, luckily, was located on the Santa Rosa High School grounds, and I often made appointments for my entire classes to go there and record their skits. Oh, did pupils enjoy being there! The professional staff taught us how to use the studio equipment. We had a student director, a sound operator, graphics technician, camera operators, floor director and, of course, talent. Then, students traded positions, so that they could record their skits and gain experience in as many areas of video production as possible.

Students learning Spanish did their skits in Spanish. Students learning English or those in Score for College did them in English. The only requirement we had when we recorded was that our projects would be played in local channels of cable television. Even parents were excited about the students being on television and seeing their names on the list of credits at the end.

What did students present? A variety of creations: Efren taught a Tae Kwon Do class. Jenny celebrated her "Quinceañera" in the studio. Others presented the songs and dances that they learned in class, vocabulary games, puppet shows, weather reports and ads.

Tears of joy flowed down my cheeks when I saw Anglo, Asian, and Mexican students holding hands as they danced to the rhythm of a Salsa melody. Languages and music have a magic for bringing together peoples of all cultures, backgrounds and social conditions.

Right along these lines, I received the unexpected, pleasant request from one of my Fourth-Year Spanish students, Brianna, when she was graduating:

"Do you think I can have the skirt I used in the dances?"

The first thought that came to mind when I heard the request was how much I had spent in buying the material and the time it took me to make those skirts, but then I thought: "It's important to her." She held it next to her heart when I said she could have it, and she left Classroom 101, displaying a big smile.

Was there any learning in these activities? Of course, and they had fun at the same time. Students practiced the target language, they planned, prepared props, learned to use video equipment, practiced leadership roles, worked in groups, dealt with a variety of cultures—very useful skills for the job market.

Students are quite creative and productive, and with dedicated students in classes, teachers avail their classroom and time for students to be creative and productive.

Mimicking the Teacher

At the end of each semester, students in Spanish as a Second Language were instructed to review the chapters that we had studied and choose a chapter from which to teach a lesson or use the vocabulary and grammatical concepts in a skit. It was a way of reviewing material for the final exam, but saying so would have sounded like work, so we called such practice "Oral Projects".

Surprise of surprises! Anita decided to teach for 20 minutes, while I took her seat among the students. It was always fun to be in the receiving end of education, especially because some students mentioned that they had never written on the board or on the plastic of the overhead projector. I made it a point to give them the opportunity to be teachers.

Anita began her presentation by turning the lights off and on as I often did to get everyone's attention. Then she asked her students to repeat after her the vocabulary words of the chapter she had chosen. She went on to teach the use of the adjective and how it must agree with the noun in gender and number. The class then made up phrases, using the vocabulary words with adjectives. The lesson ended with Anita using a puppet she had created. The puppet was playing its guitar and singing "De Colores," a song that students loved to sing for its catchy tune, with lyrics about flowers and happiness.

I truly enjoyed Anita's presentation. I saw myself in every movement that she made. It is expected that people in leadership roles will be mimicked by their followers; in a teacher's case, her students. They watch carefully the movements that we make, and then they are like mirrors that reflect with exactitude every one of our actions.

The Most Mature Class Ever

The most mature group of students I ever had was a Fourth-Year Spanish Class. They were mainly seniors, and at that level of education in a language, students are there because they want to be there, so they enjoy the activities and arrive ready to work.

My preparation style was to arrive around 7:30 a.m. and write on the side whiteboard the plan for each class, including book page numbers, exercise numbers, and everything in detail. I usually had more material than we needed, so we could have as little idle time, if any.

As I have mentioned before, in my effort "to save" as many students as possible from dropping out of school and being out in the streets, I put a lot of energy into my classes and in my personal attention to students. Naturally, I felt disappointed when in spite of my efforts, students still did not respond positively. For example, I had approached Napo in the hallway to ask him:

"Why do you miss school so much?" To which he quickly responded: "If I miss school is none of . . ."

He didn't finish his statement, but it certainly made me feel so sad.

Right after that, my Fourth-Year Spanish Class arrived, and I didn't want to cry, but I could feel my eyes becoming watery. One of the students asked me what was wrong, and that was like a call to my tears. I went to the ladies room to splash some cold water on my face to refresh myself and to calm down.

Upon return to the classroom, some students were reading the instructions on the board, and others were already working on the assignments for the day. I prepared the attendance report, delivered it to the office that was close by, so that I would get more fresh air, and when I returned, I walked around the classroom to see if there were questions. On assignments that were oral, students knew they should turn to a peer and practice the assignment. I didn't have to stand in front of the classroom during that class, and things ran smoothly.

That particular group of students made my job enjoyable. I'll keep the sweet memory of those students in my heart for ever.

If we model our expectations for youngsters, they will come through when the need arises.

The Most-Eager-to-Learn Class

I had occasion to teach regular Seniors English. In that class I had students from several countries. It sounds almost unbelievable, but the diversity was incredible. As such, most of us had an accent, and perhaps that made us feel comfortable with one another.

My literature-based approach went like this: We looked up the definition of vocabulary words that appeared in the chapter of a book we were about to read. Then we made up oral sentences with the words. Reading the chapter was next, and we took turns in reading out loud; usually I started. After reading, students answered written questions that I made up as thought-provoking as possible, either from the book or relating them to their personal experiences. They could work with a partner or two. Then we compared answers because that was another way of learning beyond the story in the book; we learned from one another's experiences.

What did we learn from one another? We learned how people among us lived, what their sufferings and joys were, what was education like in their countries of origin, geographical locations, and many other things.

Not only were my students from diverse cultures, but I had two students with learning disabilities. Thanks to them, I was assigned a Special Education teacher, Mr. Denis Tapley, who was incredibly knowledgeable, helpful, kind, and he had a great sense of humor.

In addition to reading literature, we also covered grammar, and students just loved raising their hands to give the answers. We enjoyed every moment of every day in that class.

A few years later, I attended a wedding. There, I met with one of my Godsons, who had moved away and I hadn't seen for a while.

"I want you to meet my wife, Lila," he said.

"Hello," she said looking at me to see if I would recognize her.

"You were my English teacher in my senior year," she added, and I recognized her then.

"Your love for grammar inspired me to become a secretary, and that's what I'm doing now," she shared.

"I'm glad I was able to help," I answered.

Bissell was right when she wrote: "Great thoughts are only spoken with those who meditate, but great actions are said to the entire humanity," (9). We do our best in our daily tasks, and others take off from there.

Truant Officer

At one time, there was a district Truant Officer, Mr. Eugene Mijares. The Truant Officer was important, for he saw that students were in school, and when they were not, he knew their hiding places from which he would pick them up, bring them to school, and in the evening, he would call their parents to notify them of their absences.

Why? Why go through that trouble? Well, schools receive funding for their operation, depending on the number of students in attendance every day.

I met Mr. Mijares when I had a student who would come to class once or twice a week. Thinking that he might be out in the streets causing trouble, I reported him to the Attendance Office, and the staff there asked Mr. Mijares to check into the situation. When Mr. Mijares returned from a visit to the student's home, he reported:

"You won't believe this!" He started. "Ruben stays home often because he is worried about his alcoholic mother. She sleeps when she is not drinking, and when she wakes up, she looks for more alcohol. He is afraid that she may hurt herself."

Mr. Mijares did a referral for the mother, so that she could receive the proper treatment, and he brought the student back to school.

Too bad the position of Truant Officer was eliminated in the school district due to financial problems. It was certainly a great means to assist the schools, students, and their families.

Oftentimes, we don't give teenagers the credit for being responsible, like Ruben, who sacrificed much of his education to take care of his ill mother.

The Police Officer's Teachings

In recent years, due to the violence in schools, police departments have sent police officers to schools during school hours to patrol the grounds. SRHS was no exception. One of the officers with a special ability to communicate with students, faculty, and staff was Officer Nunes.

Officer Nunes taught teachers to keep their calm when students were angry. Whether students have problems at home, they haven't passed all exams or are missing credits for graduation, some tend to arrive to class very angry.

Charles, for example, entered my English Class pushing desks aside and swearing. I remembered what the officer taught us: "Cross your arms, so that the angry student doesn't feel threatened" (Not that a petite-size teacher could intimidate anyone, but one never knows). I crossed my arms and said to him: "Charles, what's happening to you? Calm down!" Then he sat down to tell me that his *&%# counselor—wrong use of adjectives and adverbs—had told him that he didn't have enough credits to graduate. To calm him down, I said: "Your parents need to make an appointment to see the counselor with you, and that way, he can explain to you exactly what he means. If you are missing credits, he will tell you the reason, and he will suggest how you can make them up." With that, he sat down to work in class, but it was really frightening to see students angry.

"When students call you names, don't respond in an equal manner because they get angrier," Officer Nunes said. "Instead, tell them: You are probably right, but you need to pick that up, you need to do the assignment, or whatever the case may be." I tried so hard to remember his teachings and to apply them to real school situations. The tips came handy a few times.

Some Actions Should not be Punished

An unusual experience related to students being absent from my class was the morning when I received a call from the librarian.

"Mrs. Martinez, this is Laura in the library. Ryan Schmith is here. He is cutting your class and working on somebody else's assignment." I remained silent for a few second, and then I said:

"Thanks for letting me know, but I already marked him absent any way." After hanging up the telephone, I smiled as I thought: "If all cutting students were in the library working on some assignment, this world would be great." And I erased the absence.

Teacher and Facilitator

With years of experience, I noticed that students needed a facilitator as well as a teacher. For example, I gave passes to the library to those students who for one reason or another—mainly for working at night—needed to catch up with assignments in all their classes. What was my reasoning? Well, they could sit in my class worried about unfinished assignments and not pay attention to what I was trying to accomplish, or they could go take care of the work that was worrying them and return ready to listen to me and do my work. After all, most students who worked or had several extracurricular activities were responsible and interested in receiving good grades.

First and Second-year Spanish classes were on the list of courses that fulfilled the foreign language requirements for graduation. Third-year Spanish was required by some universities, so many college-bound students took it just in case the university that accepted them required it. These students knew that definitely they were going to college, and they were simply fulfilling requirements. Most of them were respectful and kind, they did all the work, and at times, they asked for extra-credit assignments, just in case they lost a few points on an exam.

I learned also to accept that some of my courses were not the most important in the students' lives or education; yet, most pupils were doing the best they could, and that was all I could ask of them. I tried to accommodate everybody's needs to their advantage.

The Chosen Ones in Score for College

Ten years of my teaching career, I was in charge of the Score for College Program. The program had been invented in Los Angeles, and I was sent there for training. Every year, I was assigned 32 students. Participation was by recommendation from teachers and counselors from middle school. They were "minority" or "disadvantaged" students with great potential to go to college. What did the program entail?

In class, we had thinking exercises, and if students had learned other mind-challenging activities in other classes, they would share them with Score. Group collaboration was included, and we did many activities in the quad or in front of the school. An example: We needed to trust one another completely, to the point that we could let ourselves fall backward from an elevated area in front of the school, and our peers would catch us by standing in two rows and holding one another's arms firmly. The exercise was also a means of learning to work as a group and to support one another. As Alarcón says, "Let's be gifts to each other, like dawns, like air, like clouds, so we can be the blue of our mutual landscapes," (10) and learn in harmony together.

Students who were in class one year became members of the Score for College Club the next, so that all students gathered at lunch time at least every other week. We had professional speakers who talked about their careers and what was necessary to become one of them.

At one time, I had an Aide, Mrs. Carmen Huerta, who visited the students' homes to let the families know how their students were doing in the program. She always took the good news of high grades and almost perfect attendance. If there was something that needed to be corrected, it was secondary news. Therefore, before her visits, she would say, "Give me positive information to take." At a later time, Mrs. Margarita Carrillo assisted me, and her style was to visit the school at unexpected times (like some parents did), to make sure that our students were in their classes.

Then administrators changed, and I no longer received the moral and economic support that I needed. There was no money for an Aide or to pay a bus to take the students on field trips to universities, so that they could see what college life was like.

I became frustrated and said to myself: "If administrators don't care, why should I?" And I allowed my own standards to deteriorate.

A Student Revived me

How did I regain confidence, energy and the drive to make the Score for College Program successful again? It was quite a lesson.

Toward the end of the first semester in a school year, Fermín, one of the chosen, went up to me to say: "I'm dropping this class. I'm not learning anything here."

His words were an awakening slap. I don't remember what class he was going to take instead, and perhaps that wasn't as important as the message he had given me. I was neglecting a class of 32 students with a potential to go to college. I wasn't living up to my own standards. I wasn't living up to the poem a parent had written to me:

"You encourage students into higher education; always there, never tiring, always with so much dedication," (11).

Whether I had the support of the administration or not, I felt it was my responsibility to guide students, so I figured out how to regain the quality of my teaching.

Instead of class sets, I bought single books on study skills, and students practiced note-taking during my lectures. I bought such materials with my own money, of course—the $35 a year that we received for each class did not amount to much. We also made a list of subjects in which students distinguished themselves. We made Tuesdays and Thursdays tutoring days, and they helped one another on a variety of topics. Everyone benefited because "In that kind of atmosphere, we empower each other to push the limits," (12).

In order to finance at least two field trips a year to universities, students practiced their planning and other leadership techniques. They had jewelry, candy, balloons and food sales to raise funds.

At one time, I rented a yellow student bus to go to U.C., Berkeley. When we arrived there, students saw other beautiful buses, and Elisa commented: "Look at those buses, and here we come, in our ghetto bus." We all thought her comment was so funny and laughed.

Elisa's comment, however, made me realize that I wasn't practicing what I was preaching. Example: "You need to start acting and dressing like the professional you want to become," was my advice. Did I want them to ride the "ghetto bus" or did I want them to experience traveling in a comfortable, luxurious bus? Yes, it was about $300 more to rent one, but "my Score kids" deserved that. From then on, we traveled in luxurious buses, and students dressed up and acted as the future professionals that they expected to become.

I began to ask students for $10 each for the field trips. I said to them: "If it's a hardship for anyone, make sure you tell me aside." All of them managed to pay $10, and the rest we paid from our fund-raisers. At the end of the school years, we even had extra money, which was deposited into our scholarship fund, and we distributed that money among the graduates each year. And to show off to the school community our progress, at the end of each semester I would make a list of "What Our Score for College Students Are Doing".

Naturally, I transferred the study skills that we practiced in Score for College to my Spanish for Spanish Speakers and Translation Courses as well. Outstanding students in those classes were also invited to attend the field trips—all thanks to Fermín's comment.

Fermín went to study in San Diego State. In one of his visits back home, he visited the Score for College Class as a speaker. He told the students about his experiences, he encouraged them not to waste their time, to work for the best grades possible, and he finished his presentation with: "Listen to Ms. Martínez. She knows what she is talking about."

His comment at the end gave me the energy and enthusiasm to keep on working and see that my students worked to their full potential; otherwise, like Charles Slack said, "If you hold yourself back, you'll never reach your dream," (13).

As hard as it is, adults have to admit that they can learn from younger generations.

A Humble Meal

It was a regular school day; noisy students waited impatiently to get out of the classroom, upon hearing the lunch-time bell. It was usually that way before lunch because teenagers were hungry. In fact, teenagers seem to be always hungry. When all students had left at 12:15, Tan entered the classroom in his usual quiet manner.

"Well, well. Look who is here!" I said as a greeting.

"Hello," he said, placing a white plastic bag on my desk. "Do you have time to eat lunch with me?" He inquired.

"Of course I do," I replied. He took out of the bag two boxes of hot Vietnamese food, the aroma of which increased my appetite and quickly filled the classroom. He handed me one of the boxes, a fork, and a soft drink—unusual lunch for a teacher. As I mentioned in other episodes, at times I didn't even get to eat. Tan and I sat on student desks, facing each other.

After the usual how-have-you-been questions and answers, he told me the purpose of his visit.

"I wanted to tell you that I received the Outstanding Educational Opportunity Program Award at Sonoma State University last week." He smiled, looked at me, and then he looked down at the floor in his humble way. "Humility, like darkness, reveals the heavenly lights," (14) said Thoreau, and the quote was the perfect description for that special moment when Tan shared his joy with me.

"Congratulations!" I said, "But why didn't you invite me to attend? Why didn't you say anything?"

"It was something small, and I know you're busy," he added.

He went on to tell me that his father had been at his graduation, and we left it at that because he had mentioned in his writings while he was my student, that he had lost his mother and sister on their way to the United States.

Tan had been one of my best and most mature students in the Score for College Program. He was attentive, kind, respectful and hard-working—all the attributes a teacher appreciates in a student. At the time of his visit, he was only in his second year at Sonoma State University, but he had accumulated most of his units for a B.S. degree in Chemistry.

When I asked him how he liked chemistry, he smiled again, and in a low voice he responded: "It's easy." His answer made me laugh because I find the sciences to be quite challenging, and to hear that chemistry was easy for him simply filled my soul with an indescribable joy.

Family Members as Students

During my first year at Santa Rosa High School, my first three children were students there. Chela was a senior about to graduate, so she had already taken the requirement for graduation. Juan did not need my class. Cheli, however, did sign up for a Spanish class with me. When students found out about our family relationship, they started to tease her with comments like: "You'll have an easy A." Being naive and not wanting to put my daughter in an uneasy situation, I asked that she be transferred to another teacher. Now I'm sorry about that because we could have worked beautifully together, like I did with Annabel and Orlando.

Five years later, and with as many years of experience, my son Rolando did enroll in one of my classes as a Teacher's Assistant. That worked very well. He helped me with attendance, paper work, and when he had extra time, he started his homework for other classes or he worked on his art projects. Art was his specialty. He was so good at it that in his senior year, he received the Aztec Plaque from California Human Development Corporation.

A sweet memory of a family member in my classroom has to do with Mercedez, my granddaughter. On Tuesdays and Thursdays, her mother, Cheli, would drop her off around 1:00 p.m. because those were our afternoons to be together. When she was about four years old, she sat on a student desk by mine, her little legs dangling down. She drew pictures or read her books, and when the bell rang at the end of class, she would say: "Class dismissed," to which all the students laughed.

Years later, my cousin Lala was placed in one of my Spanish for Spanish Speakers classes. Usually, the newly arrived students from Latin America who were placed in English as a Second Language were also assigned to my Spanish classes. It was a way of reviewing grammar in their native language, so that students could transfer that knowledge to their English language acquisition.

When Lala arrived from Mexico, I was practicing with students the skills of writing paragraphs and essays, so that, again, they could apply that knowledge when taking the writing high school proficiency exam in English. That particular day, the title of the essay was: "An Important Person in my Life."

Lala wrote and turned in her composition. She had described our grandmother Aurora as the important person in her life. Grandma had made her feel that she was the favorite granddaughter.

I could not believe my reaction. Here I was, a woman in my late 30's and feeling jealousy toward my cousin—I, too, had thought that I was grandma's favorite granddaughter. Of course, I had a hard time correcting Lala's work, but since not all writings conduced to dealing with the family, I did much better with subsequent assignments. Now I realize that all grandchildren are special to a grandmother because every time a new grandchild is born, "The great mystery blesses her again, with a part of her that enters the future . . ." (15).

Learning Responsibility from Students

It must have been midnight when the telephone rang. When I answered, the following conversation ensued:

"Mrs. Martinez, this is Ella's mother."

"Hello," I replied, half awake and yawning.

"Did you know that Ella is pregnant?"

"No, I didn't know. Is she pregnant?" At that moment, what I wanted was some rest.

"I just found out about it. I'm going to kill her right now," Mrs. Pared said.

When she said that, I became concerned, and I felt more awake.

"No, no, wait! Don't harm her," I said. After a few seconds of silence, I asked: "What did her father say?"

"He's not here. He is working. He should be arriving soon."

"Would you like me to go over to your house and tell him when he arrives?" I asked.

"That would be good," she said, perhaps as a relief of not having to face the situation on her own, but by then, I was sorry I had offered to go. I didn't want to get dressed and who knew how much time I would need to spend at their house. Without my sleep, I knew I would be useless in school the next day to the other students, so I suggested:

"Your husband may not like the idea of hearing the news from me, instead of you. Don't you think?"

"You're probably right. I'll have to tell him myself."

"If you do need me," I said, "call me back."

By then, she was calm. I knew she wasn't going to hurt her daughter, and I went back to bed. I couldn't fall asleep again. I was thinking about Ella, a 16-year old smart and lively young lady in my Score for College Program. Why would she put herself in a situation that would get her pregnant? We talked about avoiding such situations of going to the boyfriend's house or any place where the couples could be alone and engage in adults actions. But in our human nature, we are vulnerable to fall into temptation.

Early the next morning, Rod, Ella's 15-year old boyfriend, was in school eager to speak with me.

"I guess you know that Ella is expecting a baby," he commented, looking somewhat concerned and maybe afraid of my reaction.

"Yes, her mother called me last night. She is very upset," I replied.

"I know," he said, taking a deep breath. "She wants Ella to have an abortion."

"Oh, my!" I exclaimed, "She didn't say that."

"But you know?" He said as he looked at me, raising his head as if stressing his words, "I don't want that to happen. I'm going to work and go to school. I want to support Ella and our baby."

I almost fell back towards the whiteboard when he said that. He was just a child himself, and he was talking like an adult.

"She is not the first and last teenager to get pregnant," he added. "We'll start our family and figure out what to do by ourselves."

That was the end of that conversation, but he did follow through. Shortly after, they got married, the beautiful baby girl was born, and they both continued in school until they graduated from high school. By then, of course, grandma was delighted to take care of the child, while Ella and Rod went to school and worked.

Five years later, I saw the couple and their daughter. He was working as a driver in a furniture store. She had attended Santa Rosa Junior College and had completed all her general education requirements in one year. She spoke about the possibility of attending law school.

Amazing! Some young people can face the outcome of their action and move on with their dreams. "We all have lessons to learn . . . if things are easy, they are not lessons," Said Louise Hay (16).

Barb and the Graphic Designs

Often we read in the newspapers about the large percentage of teen pregnancies among the Latinas, mainly because they are not educated about their options, so I called the Sonoma County Public Health Department, asking if a speaker could visit my Spanish classes and talk about human reproduction. The person who answered my call suggested that the presentation be given to all students, for all need to be introduced to the topic that many parents avoid, mainly for not knowing how to address it.

Barb showed up on the agreed-upon date with large graphic pictures of human reproductive organs, which she clipped on the board before students arrived. Out of the 175 students I had each day, only two decided that they didn't want to hear about the topic, and I gave them passes to the library with a reading assignment.

Depending on the topic, other students asked their teachers for a pass to listen to the speakers in Classroom 101, and "Human Reproduction" was quite appealing that I had a few outsiders as listener.

All attendants were curious about what the speaker had to say. They smiled, looked bashful, giggled, but they paid attention and asked questions.

Barb spent two days with us, and two days meant 55-minute periods with each class for two days.

The first day she explained sex and how it is a normal human activity, which is more enjoyable when there's true love, especially between a married couple. Having sex simply because others are doing it creates complications, she explained.

She advised students not to make any assumptions. "Don't assume that wearing a condom is always safe. You don't know how long it has been in your partner's wallet. If pregnancy results from a casual encounter, don't assume that the father of the baby wants or doesn't want to keep it." She mentioned that having a child means having to support that child until he or she is 18.

Students had questions like: "After a woman has a child, does her vagina stay large?" To which Barb gave an educated but funny answer with a big smile: "No, mothers don't walk around with huge vaginas. The vagina enlarges to allow the baby to come out of the womb, and then it goes back to its original size." Another question was: "How can males sit down with 'that thing'?" "Well, they seem to manage," she answered.

The second day was dedicated to sexually transmitted diseases. Again, she showed them graphic pictures of people who had attended the clinic where she worked, and how the embarrassment of having to explain how they caught the disease kept people from receiving treatment right away.

She advised students to always ask with how many partners their boyfriends/girlfriends have had sex.

To avoid having to deal with unwanted pregnancies, early adult responsibilities, and the risk of catching sexually transmitted diseases, Barb advised her listeners not to practice "adult activities" before they are ready to deal with the outcome.

At the end of the presentation, students asked for Barb's business card for "their friends" to make appointments at the clinic. Alex, from my Third-year Spanish class, said to Barb and me: "This is the most informative presentation I have had about sex. Thank you!"

Barb returned for the subsequent five school years to address my students. I asked her once: "If someone questions the connection between sex education and my language and study skills classes, what should I answer?" "Life, life is the connection," she said.

To make sure that I didn't get myself and my school into trouble, I sent permission slips to students' homes, asking if it was okay for their sons and daughters to listen to the presentation. If it wasn't okay with parents, or with students themselves, like the two who did not want to listen the first time Barb presented, I usually had a story for them to read or some book exercises for them to do in the library.

Spanish as a Second Language, Translations Courses, Score for College, and all my classes encumbered topics about "life" in general, and human reproduction was one of them. Human reproduction was so well received that Lenny, one of my students in Score for College, made a follow-up research study, and then he presented his findings to the class. He stood in front of the classroom and started with: "Humans are the only mammals that have sex for pleasure. Other animals do it to preserve their species."

A University Commencement

My body shook and my teeth clattered. In the company of my husband, Juan, I attended a graduation ceremony in the outdoor Greek Theatre at U.C., Berkeley.

It was the end of May, the day had been hot in Santa Rosa, so I didn't think of taking a blanket. I figured it would be comfortable there as well. What a mistake. I was freezing, but all the discomfort was worth it. I felt honored to have received Efren's invitation to see him receive his degree in environmental science.

He was the first in his family to attend and graduate from college. In fact, he was also the first to graduate from high school. He was proving that day that with willingness and dedication, it is possible to succeed in life.

What made him a role model in high school was his respect for teachers and peers alike. In spite of being mentally gifted, he never put anyone down. On the contrary, he would arrive to the Score for College class ready to share thinking exercises or beneficial advice that he had learned in other classes or weekend workshops.

When we saw him walking up to the stage to receive his degree, we walked in the opposite direction, so that we could take a good picture of him. Then we went back to our cold, stone seat to see more graduates march through.

Next, we listened to the congratulatory speeches from educators and student speakers who recounted the hardships they had gone through in order to reach a college-level education.

When the ceremony ended, we huddled around the graduate to congratulate him. Then, Juan and I walked uphill to our automobile that would give us the much-needed warmth during our trip back to Santa Rosa. Successes need to be celebrated.

The Volleyball Trophies

Several times we were invited by the MEChA (Movimiento Estudiantil Chicano de Aztlán) Club at Sonoma State University (SSU) to participate in their annual volleyball competition. The purpose of it was to have Latino students from Sonoma County high schools visit the campus and be informed about a university education.

My students knew that they were winners and gave a lot of energy and teamwork to obtain first place in the competitions. We won first place for three consecutive years. I kept the trophies in Classroom 101.

Eventually, we noticed that we pushed and screamed at other participants in the process of winning. We were also ignoring our own peers who could not play well by not allowing them to participate, and we realized that we were not being exemplary team players. So, students and I decided that winning was not everything; our image and respect for others were more important. With that in mind, the following year we visited SSU all by ourselves, on a different day than that of the volleyball tournament. That way, we concentrated better and listened carefully to the information that our guide provided. Juan, a previous student of mine, gave us the tour at SSU. Then, Mr. Gustavo Flores, Director of Admissions, spoke to "the chosen" students himself. What a treat!

The Anonymous Helper

My colleague, Bonnie Ismael, Teacher of Special Education, confided to me one day that a certain student had been tested for level placement in English as a Second Language (ESL) classes. His score was too low, and he was sent to Special Education instead.

Her own evaluation, based on skills improvement as he learned more and more English was that he belonged in ESL. So, she requested that the Santa Rosa School District Office re-tested and reclassified him, but her requests were ignored. Andrés was a junior by the time I found out about his case.

"That's so unfair," was my reaction.

"I have tried to have him reclassified to no avail," she was sad, frustrated and angry.

An idea came to mind, and I asked her for the complete name of the student, parents' and their address. My secretarial skills came so handy—I didn't have an Associate of Arts degree in business from Santa Rosa Junior College for nothing.

I prepared a letter explaining the student's situation, Ms. Ismael called the parents to go to our school to sign it, and we sent it through regular mail. It demanded that Andrés be tested for reassignment within a two-week period. Copy: California Rural Legal Assistance (CRLA).

CRLA is a State agency that assists low-income people with civil legal cases. My sister Hilda was the Secretary there, and I knew she would bring the case to the lawyers' attention immediately. Somehow the District Office knew that, too, for shortly after, Andrés, a student from Mexico, was re-tested and reclassified to ESL classes.

I kept thinking, "How can anyone sleep peacefully, knowing that his/her negligence can make a tremendous difference in the quality of a student's life? Come to think of it, I should have gone a step farther, requesting that the negligent employee be removed from his duties. I was so thankful to have helped a youngster at Santa Rosa High School that I didn't think of others in other schools. They might have benefited from a more responsible employee.

The day of the retiring faculty luncheon, Mrs. Ismael, in charge of the event, asked if I was attending. "No, I have to prepare for final exams, compute grades, and clean up my classroom," I explained.

"Will you attend as a favor to me?" She insisted. I complied.

Oh, my goodness! When it was my turn to be thanked, Ms. Ismael handed me a framed diploma on fine school letterhead. It was signed by her and the then Principal. As I stood by her, she said: "Yolanda has made a great difference in our program. She wrote letters for parents' signatures, where they requested that students be re-tested and reclassified, after the District Office had ignored us. When she mentioned a 'legal alternative,' they immediately complied."

When I heard that, I wanted to hide. I had acted against my superiors, but I consoled myself with the thought that I was leaving, and I couldn't get fired. Besides, "Students are my priority," was my motto.

The Principal stood up and said that I had dealt with my programs and other issues without much support from the (present) administration. I knew he meant it as a compliment, but I was so hurt by that reality, and many others, that I began to cry.

When I returned to school from the luncheon, Ms. Monica Baldenegro, Assistant Principal, said, "I heard things got emotional." Although she had been so supportive and helpful to me during her first year as an administrator, I felt somewhat embarrassed at having cried, so I didn't want to go into details. I only replied: "I always get emotional." I was glad to have been of assistance to those who needed me.

Equality for Equals

When the Principal spoke about me and how I had dealt with my classes and programs on my own, he reminded me of another injustice on how students were not given the same treatment and opportunities at SRHS. "For all men cling to justice . . . justice is thought by them to be, and is, equality, not, however, for all, but only for equals," (17). I heard the injustice directly from the Principal in a meeting of the English Language Learners Committee (ESL before).

It seemed that every year, when it was time to plan for class sections for the following school year, and class sections needed to be cut back, the classes in the ELL Department were cut first. The committee asked why that was the case. I'll paraphrase the answer: Honestly, if we were to cut sections in the ArtQuest Program, parents would march in here, demanding that the sections be reinstated. What parents in ELL are going to protest? And he smiled.

Although he was right in saying that immigrants don't voice their opinions, while the ArtQuest program served the students of the affluent society—the voters, the politicians—the action itself, in my way of thinking, was inappropriate for an educator. To speak of favoritism openly was worse, and the comment truly hurt me.

The unfairness of issues at school, and being "the most indicated" to work with the Latino parents made me become quite involved with the group. At that time, the English Learners Advisory Committee had a President, Mr. Salvador Diaz, who didn't hesitate to knock on administrators' doors.

Parents began to question many things, aside from ELL class sections being reduced. They asked why administrators were cataloging all Hispanic students as gang members. They asked why they took students' pictures and placed them on their walls. They requested that students not be asked to sign any forms without their parents being present. Parents did not always receive satisfying answers, but at least it was the beginning of Latino parent involvement that would improve their sons' and daughters' circumstances at Santa Rosa High School.

CREDENTIALS AND COURSES TAUGHT

Choosing a Major

My high school counselors had advised me to go into teaching business and Spanish, but when I seriously decided to go into the Credentials Program at SSU, I said to myself: "Spanish? What challenge would that be? I'm going to major in English. English has been so difficult that I'm going to learn it well enough to teach it." I received my B.A. in English, but my college supervisor in the Department of Education, Dr. Elliott, advised: "Take the exam in Spanish, so that you are more employable." By the time I took the exam, I had been in the United States for 22 years, and the only writing I did was when I sent letters to my friends and family back in Mexico where I had come from. Fortunately, I passed the test, which included composition, grammar, reading comprehension, history, and culture.

The Love for Grammar

I passed the Spanish test because Mr. Gumaro Rivera, my Fourth-grade teacher in Mexico, had taught me "the proper use of language". He was from Pachuca, the Capital of Hidalgo State, and we were the poor kids in a town called Chicavasco. I admired his eloquence, and I learned from him to love grammar, which was a step toward the proper use of language, or languages for me years later.

Any way, in relation to English, many times I told myself: "I'll never be as good as the native English teachers." Then I heard a voice in my mind comforting me: "But you have another culture and another language that they don't have." That thought always perked me up, and I told myself: "If I can teach students to write at least as well as I do, I'll have done a great service to society." And I did. One year, three of my students participated in the League of Women Voter's writing competition, and the three received the top prizes.

Respect for my Accent

One day, while I was waiting for my turn to pay at a department store, I had occasion to speak with the lady standing behind me. She had a strong accent, and I could not keep myself from asking: "Where are you from?" She replied: "From England." I smiled as I thought: "From England, and in my ears, she has a heavy accent in English." With her answer, I remembered that people have an accent according to their countries, the regions where they come from, and the age at which they learned a new language. With that, I began to respect my accent, and I valued the great opportunity to learn more and more, every day, right along with my students.

Courses Taught

In one school year or another, during my 22 years of teaching, I taught the following courses:

First, Second, Third, Fourth and Honors Spanish Classes
English as a Second Language
Tenth Grade Academic English and 12th Grade Regular English
Spanish for Spanish Speakers, First and Second Levels
Translation courses, English/Spanish
Score for College, a Study-skills Class

When Ms. Camelli was the English Department Chair at SRHS, probably 10 years into my teaching career, I asked her if she would allow me to teach English, and she asked the Principal to assign me two sections. That meant more meetings for me because I belonged to two departments, English and Modern Languages. I had to attend both departments' meetings, and I was assigned to committees in both departments. That was a great incentive to my ego, though; I could show Anglo and Hispanic students that the language barriers can be crossed. It was a delightful time in my life! "Change is the goal in learning," (18).

Later, the Spanish for Spanish Speakers Classes came about, followed by the Translators Pathway—Yes, I was part of the committees that wrote course descriptions—and the Principal said to me: "Anyone can teach English, but I need you to teach Spanish for Spanish Speakers and the Translation Courses."

In my new assignment, we studied business terminology and wrote correspondence in both languages, and we still found the time to read classic short stories. In Mexico, I had studied business for two years, and here in the United States, I had been an Executive Secretary for 16 years. That experience gave me credit in the State of California, and my Teaching Credential was updated to reflect, besides English and Spanish, Office Service and Related Technologies. Naturally, I was feeling quite comfortable and knowledgeable, and the students respected me for that. It wasn't easy by any means, but with hours and hours of preparation, I did quite well in the complicated assignment of teaching the conjugation of verb tenses in Spanish—conditional, subjunctive in present and imperfect, present and past perfect—and whatever else came with the job of teaching Spanish for Spanish Speakers (I called it Sp3).

"The goal in education is not for teachers to pass on to students what they
know, but to discover new truths together."

ASSISTING PUPILS IN MOLDING THEIR FUTURE

I am conscientious that many of my students knew where they were going and knew how to get there, but I want to believe that my advice, words of encouragement, information or a simple letter of recommendation helped many of them reach their career goals. These are a few examples:

Tracy, physician fluent in Spanish
Robert, Disk Jockey, Artist
Alejandra, Police Officer
Dolores, Anthropologist
María, Accountant
Alberto, Banker
Norma and Angela, Restaurateurs
Tan, Chemist
Fermín, Real Estate Agent
Efrén, S.C. Board of Supervisors
José, Hispanic Religious Leader
Liliana, Lawyer

Ivonne,Silvia and Genesis, Medical Assistants
Olga, Child Development Specialist
Mariana, Sociologist
Ana Laura, Technician at H.P.
Put, Engineer, High Tech Car Systems
María Felix, Hairstylist
Susana, Mental Health Advisor
Rafael, Bank Teller
Joaquín, Teacher, Bilingual Education
Mónica, School Administrator
José, Probation Officer

Special Teachers

After Mass at Resurrection Parish, I was chatting on the patio one day, when Joaquin approached me to say hello. "What have you been doing?" I asked, and he was quick to share:

"I graduated from Sonoma State University, and I'm working now at Cali Cal Mecac Spanish Immersion School in Windsor."

I looked at him, not knowing what to say or ask, but he continued:

"You told me I could be a teacher." Such magic words! I thanked God for him having listened to me, and once more, I knew I had chosen the right profession in my life.

Healther Conchita was another teacher, but she called me one evening to say: "I want you to know that I'm abandoning the teaching profession." When I asked why she would want to do that, she mentioned the childish behavior of many teenagers these days. She said: "I can't believe that a teenager can fall off his chair, and that really bothers me." When she said that, I pictured in my mind students borrowing an eraser or a pencil from someone three rows away, reaching for it from their desks and tipping over. It's one of their favorite things to do. Besides teenagers' childish behavior, she was working for a high school in a high socio-economic neighborhood where parents demanded that their students received A's, although the students were not doing A work, or even worse, not doing work at all.

I could not blame Heather Conchita's discouragement and decision to leave the teaching profession. Nevertheless, she is still connected to education. She is working at SSU as an office employee, providing different educational services to students, with better pay and fewer headaches.

Juan, the student who gave us a tour at SSU, became an employee in the Community Media Center of the North Bay, where he gave me lessons on video production. Smiling, he said one day: "You were my teacher at one time, and now I'm teaching you." He was so proud when he said that, and I was so proud to hear him say that. I only hoped that I was as good of a student to him as he was to me.

"Mrs. Martinez, it's time we give to you; from all those students, parents, and from me, too.

We thank you and love you!" (19)

Louis became so fluent in Spanish that one day, Hispanic students asked him why he didn't have an accent when he spoke English. His answer was: "I was born here, in the United States." They continued to ask: "Why don't you have an accent when you speak Spanish?" "Because I'm always here, practicing with you, the native speakers," was his explanation. He received his teaching credential in Spanish and in mathematics. He is a private tutor in those subjects.

Other students whom I had the pleasure to teach may not have become teachers and great professionals, but they are still doing productive things in their neighborhoods. Lupita, for example, said: "I'm lucky to have a husband who is earning enough, so I can stay home to take care of my baby." She is doing society a great favor by raising her child with love and attention, helping him to take his first steps, and teaching him his first words and manners—a job with great responsibilities and greatly needed in our society. I am as proud of her as I am proud of those on the list of professionals.

WORK-RELATED RESPONSIBILITIES

When teachers mention their profession, people usually say: "You're lucky. You get out of work at 3:00 p.m." Others say: "You have the summer off."

The first comment is not correct. At 3:00 p.m. the students go home, but the teacher has to stay in school to prepare materials for the next day or to correct papers. Most of the time in my last six years of teaching, I left school at 4:00 or 4:30, and I still took home papers to correct. If papers are not corrected, students don't do the work, and they fall behind. If students fall behind, the teacher is blamed.

My daily number of students was in an average of 175, plus those in clubs. If each student turned in a homework assignment and did more written exercises during class, imagine the number of papers that needed to be collected and corrected.

Some times, students corrected their own work. Other times, they exchanged papers and corrected one another's. Yet, It's the teacher's responsibility to check the students' work, so that she can check on students' progress in the subject matter and concepts.

With time, I learned to work with packets per chapter. Students had homework and did other writing assignments in class. I went over the work, but the students of the month kept a running list of assignments. Each assignment had a number, and I collected the written work right before the chapter test. This system worked for me and for the students. Those who were absent could see on the list what exercises they had missed. Then, I decided which exercises I would review carefully. This system helped me keep my sanity to some extent. Students needed to practice responsibility in doing and keeping all the work until it was collected because the packet was worth quite a few points.

Did I mention students of the month? Every month, I recognized two students from each class, and their names were posted on the wall. They also received certificates that they took home. First I recognized the A students, and as the school year progressed, besides grades, there were always personal traits for which each student needed to be thanked: Generosity, attendance, helpfulness, etc.

Returning to "free time" that supposedly teachers have, that wasn't my experience. On Sundays, I started working around 2:00 p.m. writing lesson plans and doing whatever other preparations I needed for the following day or for the entire up-coming week.

In terms of having the summer off, yes, teachers don't have to work in the summer, unless they apply for summer school. Nevertheless, with such a heavy workload, the summer is hardly time to recharge one's energy and become healthy again. By the end of the school year, I felt my face more wrinkled and my whole body very tense.

Clubs' Advisor

Besides the Score for College Club, I was also supervisor of the MAYO (Mexican-American Youth Organization), which was culturally oriented, and we celebrated special dates like Mexican Independence Day and "Cinco de Mayo".

At one time, with Ms. Casey Elsa, I was honored to be Co-supervisor of the American Scholarship Federation. My main responsibility was to keep a record of students who had maintained a high grade point average during their high school years. On Seniors Awards Night, they received a golden cord that they proudly wore on graduation.

RECOGNITIONS

How was it that I received several recognitions as a teacher? Well, I was a great listener and, as I explained before, a facilitator. If someone had a problem, I would leave the rest of the class to go listen to him. I wasn't necessarily the students' friend, but apparently I was their confidant and a parent-type figure.

When there was a question for which I didn't have an answer, I would take it as homework, and students liked that. Also, when I made mistakes or offended someone, I would apologize, and that was how I gained the respect of my clientele—students.

By role-modeling simple manners, I managed to receive the following recognitions:

In the English Department, twice I received a letter of congratulations because students had given my name as the teacher who had inspired them the most.

Twice I received Certificates for Exemplary Dedication to Teaching from the Santa Rosa Chamber of Commerce.

Mrs. Pauline Baldenegro, parent, wrote me a poem about my dedication to students.

Erik Torres, student, wrote me a poem about my sensitivity toward students' feelings.

My students participated in several writing contests in English and in Spanish, and I received certificates of collaboration.

In the Year 2000, I received a plaque as one of 11 Outstanding Educators in Northern California.

In my office at home, there are many trinkets such as a bell and a bracelet with my name engraved on them. I have also the puppets and a blanket which students brought me from Mexico. Every item, large or small, has a special meaning.

Other cherished treasures are two thick binders full of letters of appreciation and thank-you notes.

Listing these recognitions may give the idea that I am conceited or that I want to show off, but in reality I only want to share the joy that the teaching profession offers, for certainly, no one goes into teaching for the money.

SANTA ROSA HIGH SCHOOL

Santa Rosa High School, founded in 1874, has a picturesque "Ivy League" look, with separate classroom buildings. It's a comprehensive high school, offering agriculture, automotive technologies, business, electronics, CAD drafting and wood shop. It has career pathways and partnerships with higher learning institutions.

"The core academic program is composed of courses in English, math, science, social studies, physical education and foreign languages. Foreign languages include Spanish, French and Latin. Advanced placement is available in Spanish, French, English, art, calculus, biology, chemistry, physics, economics and U.S. History. Honors credit is offered in English (freshmen, sophomore and junior), biology, chemistry, physics, government, world history, Spanish French, geometry and algebra. Physical education, required for graduation, emphasizes fitness and healthy living," (20).

Fortunately, I was able to work with students in honors, academic and regular classes. It was a great privilege to have a well-balanced workload.

SANTA ROSA, CALIFORNIA

Santa Rosa is located 55 miles north of San Francisco, in the so-called Wine Country. Santa Rosa is the pivoting point of Sonoma County, where everything comes together. "Its downtown is lined with intriguing shops and restaurants that delight casual diners and epicureans alike." (21)

Santa Rosa Junior College is conveniently located adjacent to SRHS; therefore, many students begin their general education for college during their senior year. Furthermore, Sonoma State University is located in Rohnert Park, nine miles south of Santa Rosa, making the possibility of a university education more accessible to local scholars.

The City of Santa Rosa is known as "The City Designed for Living." Its beautiful parks and recreation areas are accessible most of the year.

The Pacific Ocean is a few miles west of Santa Rosa. The Russian River has beaches in nearby locations of Sonoma County for entertainment and rest. Then, the famous giant redwood trees are farther north, along Highway 101.

Santa Rosa is in the midst of beauty and splendor.

GRADUATION—RETIREMENT

I didn't expect to "graduate" at the age of 59, but I gave so much energy to my much-loved profession that I was exhausted and ill, perhaps that's what "burned out" means.

My professional advisor said: "Leave, before they finish with you," referring to the needs and demands of all those I served.

Feeling worn out, I went to see Dr. Javier Montiel, a Naturist. He confirmed what I already knew: The problem was exhaustion. In addition to rest, I spent two months just making sure that I took my dietary supplements, so that I could bring my body up to a healthy condition again.

"We need to work on your self-esteem as well," my doctor said on my second visit.

"But . . . that was a topic I taught," I quickly responded.

"It sounds like you were giving and giving, without receiving," he explained.

On my next visit, his expert advice was:

"Don't try to solve everybody's problems. The world is the way it is. Just take care of yourself." I knew that, too, but I was acting like some of my students. They knew what needed to be done, but they dealt with other matters instead.

After I retired, my dear friends and neighbors, thinking that I might be bored at home, began to invite me to volunteer in a number of community and church activities. Job offers came my way as well, some quite tentative, such as working with small classes at local high schools. My family, however, knowing that I go beyond my boundaries when I try to help others, began to protect me. Every time I shared with them information about the offers, they asked:

"Do you remember why you left your job?" I nodded as a positive reply.

In order to stay healthy, or shall I say sane, I finally decided to do only what I can and what I like: Leading a church choir, singing in the family band, embroidering, gardening, playing my guitar, walking, reading, and writing. Some of these activities are mentally challenging and others keep me physically occupied and are great for my health.

I earned my ills and discomfort, I was proud of my accomplishments, and as hard as it was to accept it, I had to say good-bye to *Classroom 101*.

SUMMARY

"Memories of Teaching"

My school bag now rests, leaning on the left side of my desk,
with the things it had inside, when from school work I retired.

It has become part of the corner, a permanent mark and a reminder
of the sweet years I spent in school, carrying in it my teaching tools.

It's a reminder of my career: Tender smiles, occasional tears,
observing students quickly mature, enjoying their lives and some pains endure.

It's a reminder of what they shared: The youthful years we can't repair.
Their present fears and future dreams, individual stories and work in teams.

It's a reminder that I live now, off the amount that pensions allow;
the reading habit that feeds my mind; continuous learning to which I'm bound.

There it rests now, my black school bag, with the last list of students I had.
If I had to start a career once more, I would choose teaching for its
great lore.

NOTES

1. Fisher, Robert. *The Knight of Rusty Armor*, Spanish, 32nd Edition, Obelisco Editions, Barcelona, Spain, 1998, p. 62.
2. García-Davila, Armando. *At the Edge of the River*, Running Wolf Press, Healdsburg, CA, 2001, p. 4.
3. Hay, Louise L. *You Can Heal Your Life*, Spanish, Litografía Cozuga, Mexico City, 2007, p. 75.
4. Ibid, p. 59.
5. Dodd, Robert C. Quote in *Light for my Path*, Barbour Publishing, Inc., Wheaton, IL, 1999, p. 132.
6. van Zeller, Hubert. Quote in *Light for my Path*, p. 112.
7. Slack, Charles. "We are all Here to Learn," a story in *Chicken Soup for the Woman's Soul*, Spanish, Health Communications, Inc., Deerfield Beach, FL, 1997, p. 170.
8. Hay, p. 126.
9. Bissel, Emily P. *Chicken Soup for a Woman's Soul*, p. 24.
10. Alarcón, Francisco X. Poem "Let's Gather up These Mornings," *Madness and Other Misfortunes,* Creative Arts Book, Co., Berkeley, CA, 1999, p. 29.
11. Baldenegro, Pauline. Parent, Santa Rosa High School, single poem, "Thank-you, Mrs. Martinez," 2006.
12. Rivera, Auti. "Pushing the Limits," article in *Latina Magazine,* June-July 2012 issue, p. 58.
13. Roosevelt, Eleanor. Quote in *Chicken Soup for a Woman's Soul*, p. 170.
14. Thoreau, Henry David. Quote in *Light for my Path*, p. 98.
15. Whitaker, Kay Cordell. "About Childbirth," story, *Chicken Soup for a Woman's Soul*, p. 219.
16. Hay, p. 66.
17. Ross, W.D., Editor. *Aristotle Selections*, Charles Scribner's Sons, N.Y., 1955, p. 303.
18. Maxwell, John. *How to Win People,* Spanish, Nelson Group, Nashville, TN, 2004, p. 99.
19. Baldenegro
20. www.srcs.k12.ca.us, Santa Rosa High School.
21. www.santarosachamber.com, Santa Rosa, California.